CHAIN REACTIONS

From Sea Urchins to Dolly the Sheep

Discovering Cloning

Sally Morgan

Heinemann
LIBRARY

www.heinemann.co.uk/library

Visit our website to find out more information about Heinemann Library books.

To order:
Phone 44 (0) 1865 888066
Send a fax to 44 (0) 1865 314091
Visit the Heinemann Bookshop at www.heinemann.co.uk/library to browse
our catalogue and order online.

Produced for Heinemann Library by
White-Thomson Publishing Ltd,
Bridgewater Business Centre,
210 High Street,
Lewes, East Sussex BN7 2NH

First published in Great Britain by Heinemann Library,
Jordan Hill, Oxford OX2 8EJ, part of Harcourt Education.

Heinemann Library is a registered trademark of Harcourt
Education Ltd.

Consultant: Michael Reiss
Commissioning editor: Andrew Farrow
Editors: Kelly Davis and Richard Woodham
Proofreader: Catherine Clarke
Design: Tim Mayer
Picture research: Amy Sparks
Artwork: Wooden Ark

Originated by RMW
Printed and bound in China by South China
Printing Company

10 digit ISBN 0431185948
13 digit ISBN 978 0 431 18594 1
10 09 08 07 06
10 9 8 7 6 5 4 3 2 1

British Library Cataloguing in Publication Data
Morgan, Sally
From sea urchins to Dolly the sheep : discovering cloning
- (Chain reactions)
660.6'5
A full catalogue record for this book is available from the
British Library.

Acknowledgements. The author and publisher would like
to thank the following for allowing their pictures to be
reproduced in this publication:
Corbis pp. 1 (Bluestone), 4 (Seoul National
University/Reuters), 18 (Clouds Hill Imaging Ltd/David
Spears), 19 (Chris Collins), 23 (Annie Griffiths Belt),
27 (Najlah Feanny), 42–43 (Jim Richardson), 45 (Craig
Connor), 47 (Rick Friedman), 51 (Reuters/Larry Downing),
53 (Dave G. Houser/Post-Houserstock), 55 (Pierre-Paul
Poulin/Magma/Sygma); Ecoscene pp. 6 (Phillip Colla),
9 (Phillip Colla), 15 (Robert Pickett), 16 (Robert Pickett),
39 (Fritz Polking); Index Stock Imagery pp. 48–49; Photo
Library/Oxford Scientific Films pp. 11 (David M. Dennis),
12, 38 (Stan Osolinski); Science Photo Library pp. 5 (Helen
McArdle), 10, (Edelmann), 13 (Jim Zipp), 14 (David
Aubrey), 20 (James King-Holmes), 22 (Novosti),
24 (Maximilian Stock Ltd), 25 (Volker Steger), R.L.
Brinster, Peter Arnold Inc.), 29 (James King-Holmes),
(Ph Plailly/Eurelios), 34 (John Mclean), 35 (J.C. Revy),
36 (Andrew Leonard), 37 (Simon Fraser/Royal Victoria
Infirmary, Newcastle upon Tyne), 41 (David Aubrey),
46 (Mauro Fermariello), 52 (AJ Photo), 54 (Bluestone),
cover and 31 (PH. Plailly/Eurelios); Topfoto.co.uk pp. 17,
32 (Fastfoto Picture Library), 33 (Fastfoto Picture Library),
40 (Keystone).

Cover design by Tim Mayer.

Every effort has been made to contact copyright holders
of any material reproduced in this book. Any omissions
will be rectified in subsequent printings if notice is given
to the publishers.

Contents

Any words appearing in the text in bold, **like this**, are explained in the Glossary.

Making copies

Snuppy looks like a perfectly normal Afghan dog. But he is very special. He is the world's first cloned dog and he is an exact copy of another dog. Cloning was once only found in science fiction. For instance, there are armies of clones in the film *Star Wars Episode II: Attack of the Clones*. But now science fiction is quickly becoming science reality. Some scientists may one day try to clone famous people, such as Elvis Presley, or animals that have died out, such as the dodo.

Snuppy (right) was cloned from the skin cell of an adult Afghan hound (left) in 2005. Snuppy was cloned in Korea by Professor Woo Suk Hwang and his team. Much of Hwang's research has since been discredited, but Snuppy was found to be a genuine clone.

Cloning in nature

Cloning means making exact copies of **organisms**. It occurs naturally in the world around us. For example, identical twins are clones of each other. Gardeners take cuttings of plants to make new plants, and this is also a form of cloning. However, scientists are now able to make clones of animals such as frogs and sheep.

Imagine you had a prize-winning racehorse. You might want to breed other horses from it, but the offspring might not be as good. This is because each foal would inherit characteristics from both parents. Cloning gets around this problem because all the offspring are exactly the same. This means, for instance, that farmers could one day clone their best dairy cows. Pet owners could also clone their pets.

The British scientist, J.B.S. Haldane, was the first person to use the word "clone" in 1963. It was a Greek word that meant "twig". He made a speech describing his vision of a world where cloning humans would be possible. He said that the best and brightest people would be cloned and that this would improve the human race.

The story of cloning

The cloning story began about a hundred years ago, when scientists started studying how animals reproduce themselves. They began by looking at simple organisms, but soon they moved on to frogs and newts.

Cloning experiments are very difficult to carry out. At one point, scientists believed it would never be possible to clone a **mammal**. But they were proved wrong. One day, cloning may be used to help people suffering from diseases such as Parkinson's and **leukaemia**.

This book traces the steps in the history of cloning. Each step was a challenge. There were a lot of successes and just as many failures along the way. The story of cloning is still continuing today. There has been a lot of debate, among scientists, politicians, and the general public, about the rights and wrongs of these new techniques. This book discusses some of these difficult issues.

Identical twins are natural clones of each other.

5

The beginnings of cloning

The first step in the cloning story dates back to the 1890s. At this time, scientists were observing cells using a light microscope. They were studying the way cells divide to form new cells. Scientists knew that hereditary information must pass from the parent cell to the daughter cell. They believed that this information was located in the cell's **nucleus**. This information was needed to tell the new cell how to grow and function.

The chain of events began with a German scientist called Hans Driesch (1867–1941), who carried out experiments on sea urchins. Driesch was interested in the way hereditary information was passed between cells. Other scientists thought that some of the information was lost when a cell divided. Driesch did not believe this, and wanted to prove it wrong.

The sea urchin belongs to a group of marine animals called echinoderms, meaning "spiny-skinned" animals.

Driesch decided to work on sea urchin **embryo** cells because they were large and therefore easier to see than other types of cell. He took a sea urchin egg that had just divided into two cells. He then placed it in a beaker of seawater, and shook it until the two cells separated.

The two cells were left floating in the seawater, and each one grew into a new sea urchin. The two sea urchins were identical. Driesch had produced clones. He had also proved that the hereditary information had not decreased in any way.

Driesch's experiment involved splitting an embryo. A similar process takes place naturally with identical twins. When an embryo divides into two, identical twins are formed.

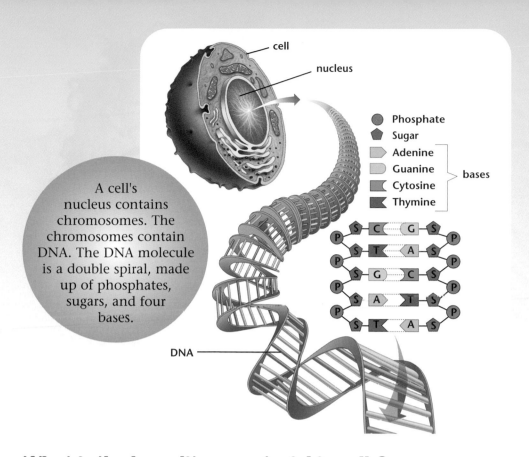

A cell's nucleus contains chromosomes. The chromosomes contain DNA. The DNA molecule is a double spiral, made up of phosphates, sugars, and four bases.

cell

nucleus

Phosphate
Sugar
Adenine
Guanine
Cytosine
Thymine

bases

DNA

What is the hereditary material in cells?

The nucleus is one of the largest structures in a cell. Inside the nucleus are long, thread-like **chromosomes**. The chromosomes contain **DNA (deoxyribonucleic acid)**. DNA is the chemical that holds the **genetic code** for a living thing. A **gene** is a specific length of DNA, and there can be hundreds of genes on a single chromosome. During the first half of the 20th century, scientists proved that DNA carried the hereditary information from one cell to the next.

? WHAT IS DNA?

The structure of the DNA **molecule** was worked out in 1953 by two scientists called Francis Crick and James Watson. DNA is made up of three components: sugars, phosphates, and nitrogen-containing compounds called **bases**. There are four types of bases, and the sequence of bases along a length of DNA forms the genetic code. This code contains the instructions needed to make proteins.

Cloning newts

Another German scientist, Hans Spemann (1869–1941), was also doing experiments with embryos. He was working with newts, a type of tailed amphibian related to frogs and salamanders. In 1901, Spemann performed a very similar experiment to the one that Hans Driesch had carried out a few years earlier. Spemann took a newt's egg that had divided into two cells. He then separated each cell into two parts. The two parts grew into identical newts. Again, this proved that both cells contained all the hereditary information needed to grow into a healthy individual.

Producing a clone

In 1914, Spemann carried out another experiment, using a technique that was to become very important in cloning. He took a newly **fertilized** newt's egg before it had divided into two cells. He then wrapped a strand of baby hair around the middle of the cell. By tightening the loop of hair, he could force the nucleus to one side of the cell. This left just the **cytoplasm** (gel-like material) on the other side. The nucleus divided repeatedly. Soon there were several nuclei on one side of the cell. One of these nuclei then slipped across to the empty side of the cell, where it started to divide. Spemann had managed to transfer a nucleus and create two individuals from one cell.

Natural cloning

Cloning occurs naturally in the living world, mostly in plants and among the simpler animals. It is not normally called cloning. Instead, it is known as **asexual reproduction**. This is a form of reproduction that involves only one parent.

THAT'S AMAZING!

Under ideal conditions, a single **bacterium** can divide to form more than 2 million bacteria in just seven hours.

Some animals and plants reproduce asexually when they want to increase their numbers quickly – for instance, when there is plenty of food and space. By using asexual reproduction, one individual can produce lots of copies of itself in a short time. All the offspring are identical to the parent **organism**.

In good conditions, a single bacterial cell can divide into two new cells. After about 20 minutes, each of the two cells is ready to divide again, and then again. Yeast, a type of fungus, usually reproduces asexually by budding. A bud appears on the side of the cell, gets larger, and then breaks off.

The hydra, a simple animal related to the sea anemone, also reproduces by budding. Just like the yeast, a bud appears on the side of its body and grows into a new hydra.

The type of sea anemone shown here produces buds under its tentacles that grow into small anemones. The offspring live on the parent until they slide off and become independent anemones.

Embryos

An embryo is produced by **sexual reproduction** when a sperm fertilizes an egg cell. Sexual reproduction involves two parents. Unlike asexual reproduction, the offspring are different from the parents because they inherit features from both of their parents.

The fertilized egg divides to form two identical cells. The two cells grow. Then, after a short while, they divide to form 4 cells, and then 8, 16, 32, 64, 128, and so on. Soon there is a ball of cells that are all identical. After about 14 days, the cells start to specialize. This means that they develop into different types of cells. For example, some become skin cells, while others form liver, muscle, or blood cells. During this process, the cell may undergo structural changes. For instance, red blood cells lose their nucleus.

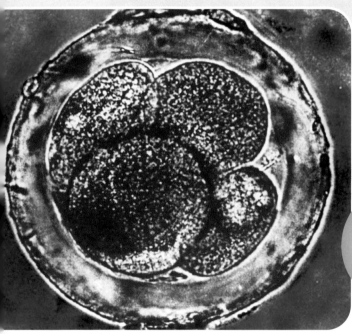

This is an embryo at the four-cell stage.

HOW MANY CHROMOSOMES IN AN EMBRYO?

Most human cells have 46 chromosomes. However, the **gametes** (eggs and sperm) contain only 23 chromosomes each. If the gametes contained 46 chromosomes they would fuse together to produce a cell with 92 chromosomes. During the production of gametes, the chromosome number is therefore halved. The embryo contains 46 chromosomes, with 23 coming from the egg and 23 from the sperm.

Specialized cells

Towards the end of his life, Spemann was thinking about the process of cell specialization. He wanted to know whether a nucleus from a specialized cell still contained all the hereditary information needed to grow and develop a new individual. Or, to put the question another way, did the nucleus lose all the hereditary information as the cell changed and became specialized?

In 1938, Spemann suggested an experiment that would answer his question. He called it a "fantastical experiment". He wanted to remove an intact nucleus, with all its hereditary information, from an adult cell of a newt. He would then place this nucleus in an egg cell that had had its own nucleus removed. He wanted to see if he could get the egg cell with its new nucleus to grow into an adult. If the experiment was successful, it would prove that a specialized adult cell still had all the information needed to make a new healthy individual.

Sadly, Spemann died a few years later, in 1941, and never got the chance to perform this experiment. It would not be successfully carried out until 1952, by two scientists called Robert Briggs and Tom King (see page 14).

This is a cave salamander. Newts and salamanders are tailed amphibians. Spemann probably chose them for his experiments partly because they lay large eggs.

Cloning frogs

Hans Spemann proposed his "fantastical experiment" in 1938. However, the world was soon thrown into chaos by the Second World War (1939–1945), and biological research was disrupted during much of the 1940s. There were no major advances in cloning until 1952, when Robert Briggs (1911–1983) and his team, working in Philadelphia, in the United States, succeeded in cloning a frog **embryo**.

This is a common frog tadpole. Its back legs are starting to form.

A fantastical experiment

Robert Briggs was interested in the way a frog embryo developed into a tadpole and then changed into an adult frog. This process is called **metamorphosis**. He was particularly interested in the role of the **nucleus** and the **chromosomes**. There was still a great debate going on about whether hereditary information was lost as cells became specialized.

After many years of working with frog embryos, Briggs felt he was ready to carry out a similar experiment to the one suggested by Hans Spemann to prove whether information was kept or lost. He decided to take a nucleus from an embryonic frog cell. He then planned to insert it into an unfertilized egg cell that had had its nucleus removed. Many of his fellow researchers felt this was a foolish idea that was bound to fail. Even Briggs was unsure about whether he would succeed in performing this technically difficult procedure.

Briggs worked with Tom King who had done a course in microsurgery, an essential skill for this experiment. Before they could start the experiment, the team had to make their tiny tools, including special glass needles and pipettes (hollow glass tubes for sucking up liquid). They planned to carry out the whole experiment under a very powerful light microscope.

WHAT IS METAMORPHOSIS?

Amphibians, such as frogs and toads, can live on land and in water. They go through several changes in their life cycle. This process of change is called metamorphosis. The female frog or toad lays eggs that are **fertilized** by the male. The eggs hatch into tadpoles. Tadpoles live in the water and they have external gills and a long tail. During the next couple of months, a tadpole's body goes through a series of changes. First, the external gills become covered by a flap so they are internal. Then the gills are replaced by lungs. Next, the legs appear. Finally the tail gets absorbed into the body, and the young amphibian is ready to leave the water. The adult frogs and toads live mainly on land.

frog

tadpole with
back legs

tadpole

embryo

egg

Nuclear transfer

The experiment carried out by Briggs and King was in three parts. First, they had to remove a nucleus from an unfertilized egg cell. Then they had to get a nucleus from an embryonic cell. Lastly, they had to insert the nucleus from the embryonic cell into the empty egg cell. They hoped the cell would then start to grow and divide. They believed it would eventually form a frog that was identical to the one growing in the original embryo.

Briggs and King took a frog's egg. Using their tiny scissors, they made a cut in the jelly layer around the egg. They sucked out the nucleus. Then they took an embryo and pulled it apart, separating the cells. Somehow they had to remove the nucleus from one of these cells. They used a special glass pipette. The diameter of the pipette was deliberately smaller than the cell. They sucked gently on the pipette, pulling the cell partly into the tube. The cell **membrane** broke and the nucleus popped into the tube. With the nucleus still in the tube, the scientists inserted the pipette into the empty egg cell and dropped the nucleus inside.

Robert Briggs used embryos of the northern leopard frog, a type of spotted frog common in ponds in North America.

This frog embryo is starting to lengthen and take on the appearance of a tadpole.

Success at last

At first the experiment failed because the embryos kept dying, but the two scientists kept on trying. Eventually they managed to get one embryo to survive and grow. There was great excitement in the laboratory, and soon other scientists were visiting to see the embryo. Then disaster struck. One of the visiting scientists squashed the embryo with a pair of forceps! Fortunately, Briggs and King were able to repeat their success a few weeks later. In total, they transferred nuclei into 197 egg cells. Of these, 104 started to develop, of which 35 survived to become proper embryos, and 27 developed into tadpoles.

This was the first time that nuclear transplantation had been performed. Scientists from around the world visited Robert Briggs' laboratory and learned how to carry out this technique. Now known as **nuclear transfer**, this method is still used today, although there have been a few changes in the way it is performed. It was a major breakthrough and enabled scientists to make great advances in cloning, as will be explained in the following chapters.

TALKING SCIENCE

"We got a good deal of reaction, from both scientists and non-scientists. They thought it was phenomenal. We thought we could clone any cell."
Tom King, in *Clone*, by Gina Kolata (1997)

From adult cell to embryo

The successful cloning experiment carried out by Briggs and King in 1952 had used a nucleus taken from an embryo at an early stage of development. Then they attempted to carry out nuclear transfers with progressively older cells. However, as the cells became specialized, it became more and more difficult to produce clones. Had the **DNA** somehow changed so that it could no longer be cloned?

The next step forward was taken by John Gurdon, at Oxford University, UK. He used the African clawed toad for his experiments. He chose this type of toad because it matured quickly, so researchers would soon know whether the cloning had worked.

In 1962, Gurdon repeated the Briggs and King experiment, using a nucleus from a cell taken from an adult frog's gut lining. After many attempts, he reported that the experiment had been successful. He had obtained tadpoles by transferring an adult cell's nucleus into a frog's egg. This proved that the genetic information was not lost or changed. If the genetic information had been altered, the new cell would not have been able to develop into a tadpole. Gurdon concluded that an adult cell had all the genetic material needed for a new individual to develop.

African clawed toads are really frogs. They are found in freshwater streams and lakes in Africa. They have long been a popular laboratory animal.

Most of the media reports about the work of Gurdon, Briggs, and King described cloning as a good thing. This was a time when science was making great progress. For example, the American astronaut Neil Armstrong had just walked on the Moon. People thought that science was going to make life better for everyone. This was very different from the later debate about the rights and wrongs of cloning, which would result from the research of the 1980s and 1990s.

Poor success rate

The success rate of Gurdon's experiment was very low. Only 2 out of every 100 nuclear transfers were successful. Gurdon blamed this high failure rate on the fact that the nuclei were damaged as they were sucked out of the adult cell and squeezed into the egg cell. But there was another problem. The tadpoles did not change into frogs, and no one knew why. Tadpoles cloned from embryonic cells grew into adults, but those cloned from adult cells did not develop into adults.

When John Gurdon published the results of his work with clawed toads, it created a great deal of excitement in the scientific community. But there were some who tried to find fault with his research.

At the same time, some other scientists were trying out this method of cloning using mice. Again, the mouse embryos produced using nuclei from adult cells did not grow into adult mice. This was a major stumbling block. It seemed to show that adult cells did not have all the genetic information needed to direct the development of a new individual after all.

Cloning mammals — an impossible challenge?

By the late 1970s, scientists were wondering if it would ever be possible to clone a mammal. There had been thousands of cloning experiments on frogs and mice, but most had failed. No one had managed to clone an adult cell and grown it to maturity.

Three mice

Then, in 1979, a scientist in Germany, Karl Illmensee, announced that he had cloned three mice. His research attracted international media attention. Illmensee had used a similar method to the one used by Briggs and King. He took a mouse **embryo**, pulled the cells apart, and removed the **nucleus** from one of the cells. Then, he said, he had removed the nucleus from an egg cell and replaced it with an embryonic nucleus in one swift movement. Three embryos had been produced in this way. They had been placed in the **uterus** of a female mouse. There, they had developed normally into baby mice. The baby mice were clones of the embryo from which the nucleus had been taken.

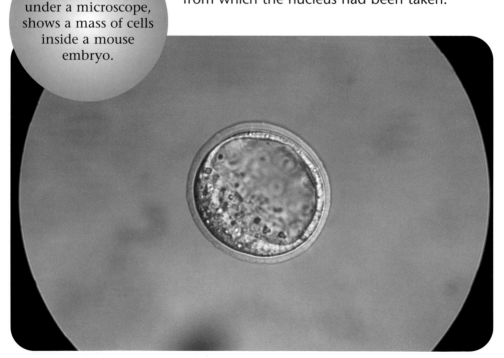

This photograph, taken under a microscope, shows a mass of cells inside a mouse embryo.

There were headlines in all the newspapers and soon Illmensee was lecturing around the world. However, after all the excitement had quietened down, scientists began to look more closely at his research. It was revealed that nobody had ever seen Illmensee carry out a **nuclear transfer**, not even the people who were working in his laboratory. Errors were discovered and Illmensee admitted to being careless when recording dates and procedures. Soon Illmensee's reputation was in tatters.

Mice are popular laboratory animals because they breed rapidly, and they are small and inexpensive to keep.

In 1983, Davor Solter and James McGrath tried to repeat Illmensee's work. They cloned mice using the nuclear transfer method. After many failed attempts, they concluded that it was impossible to clone mammals using the technique Illmensee had described.

Cloning got a lot of bad publicity after the Illmensee affair. There was little money available for cloning research and many scientists turned their attention to the development of new **genetic engineering** techniques instead.

? WHAT IS A SCIENTIFIC PAPER?

Scientists publish their research as an article, known as a paper, in scientific journals. The paper records all the experimental methods that were used and all the results. Other scientists can then test the research by carrying out the same experiments themselves. They will try to get the same results, using the same methods. Sometimes it is useful to publish a paper with negative results (in other words, an experiment that does not work). Davor Solter and James McGrath published their paper to prove that cloning mammals was impossible using Illmensee's technique. Even though they were using the same methods as Illmensee, they got negative results every time.

The race to clone a mammal

A few scientists continued to work on cloning, despite all the negative publicity and the lack of funding. The next breakthrough came in the mid-1980s when two research teams announced that they had cloned a mammal. The two teams were working separately, but they were using similar methods. One team was led by Steen Willadsen in the United Kingdom, and his team was working on sheep embryos. The other team was led by Neal First, based at the University of Wisconsin, in the United States. The American scientists were working on embryos from cows.

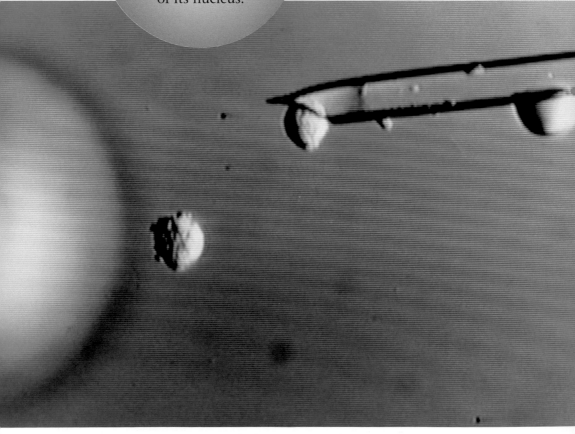

In this photograph, a pipette is being used to suck up an embryonic sheep cell. The cell is then injected into a sheep's egg that has been emptied of its nucleus.

The two teams were having problems with their experiments. Then they both saw an advertisement in a science magazine called *Nature*. It was advertising a machine that fused cells together, using a tiny burst of electricity. Without realizing it, both teams bought the same machine. It gave them the breakthrough they had been looking for.

Embryo cloning

Steen Willadsen did a lot of research into embryos before starting on cloning. He found he could pull embryos into two pieces and each one would grow into a healthy individual, just as Hans Driesch had done almost 100 years earlier. The new individuals were clones of each other, but they were different from the parents. This method was called embryo cloning.

However, Willadsen found that there was a much higher success rate if the embryo was pulled into only two pieces. If the embryo was pulled into 8 or 12 pieces, the success rate went down sharply. This research was valuable because Willadsen found out a lot more about embryos.

Willadsen wanted to produce lots of offspring from one embryo, not just a few by embryo cloning. He decided to separate all the cells of an embryo. He would then place each embryo cell in an empty egg cell. This way, he could make many clones of the embryo.

WHAT METHOD DID WILLADSEN USE?

Willadsen started by using Karl Illmensee's method. But it did not work, so he developed his own technique. The previous researchers had used **fertilized** egg cells because they believed it was important for the egg to have been fertilized. Willadsen decided to use unfertilized sheep's eggs as the recipients. He removed their nuclei. Then he fused each embryonic cell with one of the empty egg cells. To do this, he used a burst of electricity produced by the machine he had bought. It worked. He grew the resulting embryos in the laboratory. Next, he implanted them into the uterus of a **surrogate** sheep. His first lambs, cloned by nuclear transfer, were born in 1984.

Cloning cattle

In the United States, Neal First wanted to make clones of cattle. Embryos produced from the best cows could be sold for a great deal of money. It therefore seemed a good idea to try to produce lots of embryos from a single cow embryo.

He started by practising nuclear transfer on mouse embryos, using a method similar to the one described by Illmensee. But the cells kept dying and Neal First's team could not work out why. They decided to use their new electrical machine to fuse the embryonic cell with the egg cell. Using this method, they succeeded in getting a cloned embryo. This embryo was implanted into a cow. Ten months later, a calf was born.

A researcher holds two cloned rabbits produced at a breeding centre in Russia.

Within a short time, researchers elsewhere had cloned horses, pigs, rabbits, and goats. However, in all these experiments, the source of the nucleus was an embryo. They had not tried to clone an adult cell. That was the next challenge that awaited scientists working on cloning.

WHAT ARE HUMAN SURROGATES?

The first human mother-to-mother embryo transfer took place in Australia in 1982. Since that time, many women have given birth to babies for infertile couples who cannot have children of their own. These women are acting as surrogate mothers. The baby is usually handed over to the parents within days of birth. Some women are paid to be surrogate mothers. In other cases, a woman may agree to have a baby for a friend or family member who cannot have children of her own. Some people think there is nothing wrong with human surrogacy, while others believe that it should not be allowed.

Surrogate mothers

In many of the nuclear transfer experiments, the embryo is placed in the uterus of an unrelated female animal, where it develops into a new individual. This is known as mother-to-mother embryo transfer.

This procedure was developed for use in cattle in the 1950s when a **hormone** called FSH (follicle stimulating hormone) became available. This hormone causes the cow to release a large number of eggs from her **ovaries**. The cow is then **artificially inseminated** with sperm to fertilize the eggs. A few days later, her uterus is washed out to retrieve the embryos. The embryos are checked under a microscope. Then the healthy ones are implanted into the uteruses of other cows. A cow that receives an embryo is called a surrogate.

A surrogate is usually a female of the same species. More recently, scientists involved in cloning rare animals have used surrogates of a closely related species (see page 38).

This grandmother (right) acted as a surrogate mother for her own grandchildren because her daughter (left) was born without a uterus. The two women, from South Dakota, in the United States, are shown here with the nine-month-old twins in 1992.

The road to Dolly the sheep

While researchers were trying to succeed with cloning, a lot of exciting research was being done on **genetic engineering**. The science of genetic engineering involves altering **DNA**. Scientists soon learned how to insert a new piece of DNA into the DNA of bacteria and yeast. This enabled the **bacterium** or yeast cell to make a new protein. Then they wanted to genetically modify the DNA of mammals, such as sheep.

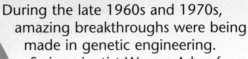

Fermentation units are used to grow genetically modified bacteria. The red liquid is full of nutrients that are used by the bacteria. Some bacteria are genetically modified in order to produce medical drugs, which can be extracted from the liquid.

During the late 1960s and 1970s, amazing breakthroughs were being made in genetic engineering. Swiss scientist Werner Arber found some chemicals, called restriction **enzymes**. These chemicals acted like biological scissors. They could snip the DNA at certain places, while other types of enzymes joined the ends back up again. Soon scientists could remove a length of DNA, using a restriction enzyme. They could then insert it into another piece of DNA, rather like cutting and pasting in a computer programme.

Scientists altered the DNA of bacteria to enable them to make new proteins. These bacteria were called genetically modified (GM) bacteria because their genetic information had been changed. One of the most important genetic alterations gave bacteria the ability to make human insulin. This is a protein that is needed by people suffering from **diabetes**.

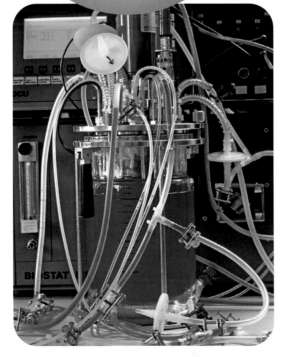

Many different genetically modified **organisms** were produced, including bacteria, yeasts, and plants. Soon scientists were thinking about modifying mammals. At this point, genetic engineering and cloning came together. If scientists could produce a genetically modified mammal, it would be very valuable. They would then want to breed from it. However, if they allowed a genetically modified animal to breed naturally, there was no guarantee that the offspring would inherit the new ability. Cloning would solve the problem. They could clone the parent animal, so that the offspring were identical.

The hepatitis B vaccine is given to prevent the disease hepatitis, which damages the liver. The vaccine is produced using GM bacteria. Here, a technician at a biotechnology company in India checks the quality of a sample of vaccine.

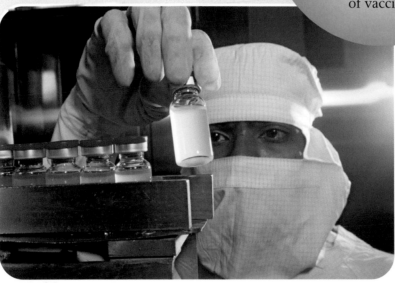

? WHAT ARE ENZYMES?

Enzymes are made of protein. There are thousands of different types of enzymes in cells. They increase the speed at which chemical reactions take place. Each enzyme is only involved with one type of reaction. For example, saliva contains the enzyme salivary amylase. This enzyme's role is to speed up the rate at which starch in food is broken down into sugar. Several enzymes are essential for genetic engineering. These include the restriction enzymes that chop up DNA, DNA polymerase that is involved in making new DNA, and DNA ligase that joins up lengths of DNA.

Genetically modifying sheep

In 1981, a scientist called Ian Wilmut started adding a **gene** to **fertilized** sheep's eggs in order to produce a **genetically engineered** sheep. Sheep with this gene would produce milk containing a drug that was called alpha-1 antitrypsin. This drug could be used to treat inherited lung diseases.

First, Wilmut had to work out how to insert the gene into the fertilized egg. If he succeeded, the gene would be absorbed by the egg's **DNA** and would be present in every cell of the animal's body. Then he would have to ensure that the new gene was only activated (switched on) in the cells of the udder where the milk was made.

The mouse on the right has been genetically altered so that it produces a rat growth **hormone**. As a result, it has grown to twice the size of a normal mouse. This technique could be used to increase meat production in farm animals.

SELECTIVE BREEDING VERSUS GENETIC ENGINEERING?

Farm animals have been bred over many generations to produce animals with desirable characteristics, such as lean meat or high milk yield. Genetic engineering offers a short cut. The DNA can be changed, and the change happens straight away. It can also be controlled to a greater extent, whereas selective breeding may not always work. The parents may have the right characteristics, but the offspring may have a different combination of features. DNA from other species can also be incorporated, using genetic engineering.

Wilmut started by removing the desired gene from human DNA using restriction **enzymes**. He made many copies of the gene. Then the DNA was sucked up and injected into a fertilized egg. He hoped that the new strand of DNA would be absorbed into the DNA in the cell **nucleus**. However, this process proved to be very difficult, and most of the **embryos** died. Only 1 or 2 in every 1,000 absorbed the gene. These embryos were placed in the **uterus** of a ewe, where they developed into lambs. The lambs then grew into sheep that made the drug alpha-1 antitrypsin in their milk.

Professor Ian Wilmut is shown here in his laboratory, at the Roslin Institute in Scotland.

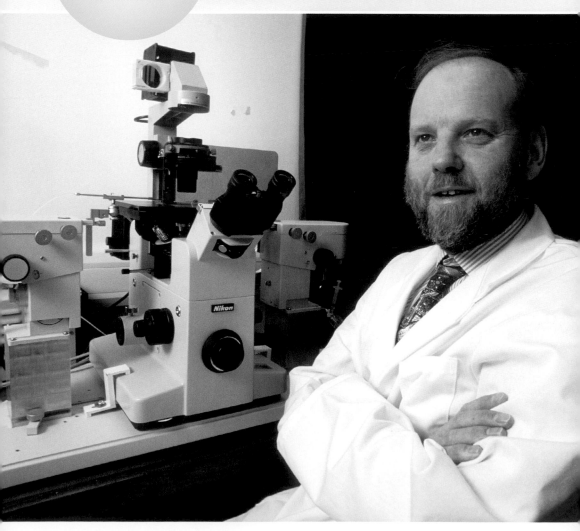

Improving the technique

Although he had successfully produced genetically modified sheep, Wilmut's success rate was still very low. He therefore decided to try a different method.

He grew vast sheets of embryonic cells in the laboratory. He then flooded these sheets of cells with the DNA, rather than injecting them one by one. He tricked the cells into absorbing the DNA by giving them a small electric shock. The shock forced open tiny pores in the cell **membrane** and allowed the DNA to enter the cells. Wilmut then tested the cells to see which ones had taken in the DNA. Then he transferred the altered nuclei into empty eggs.

However, Wilmut was using cells taken from embryos that were just a few days old and he could not get them to grow. In 1987, he decided to use cells from an embryo that was nine days old. He realized that he could grow these cells, and then clone them.

Cell cycles

Wilmut decided to work with another scientist, called Keith Campbell, on the cloning part of the process. Campbell had studied the way DNA behaves when cells divide. After a cell has divided, it goes through a growth stage when the cell enlarges. This phase can last for any period of time – hours, days, or even years. Then it gets ready to divide again. At this point, it makes new supplies of proteins and other substances. It also copies all its DNA so that it has double the usual amount. Then it goes through another growth phase, in which it builds up its energy stores. After this, it divides into two.

THAT'S AMAZING!

Ian Wilmut decided to carry out his research on sheep, rather than cows, because sheep were very cheap in Scotland! He could get 100 sheep for the price of one cow.

Most researchers did not pay much attention to the cell cycle when they removed a cell nucleus. However, Campbell thought there might be a problem if a nucleus was removed from a cell at one stage in the cell cycle, and then inserted into a cell at a different stage. He decided to starve all his cells so that they would stop growing and dividing and go into a resting state. Then he would clone them. This simple idea worked, although it took Wilmut and Campbell eight years to find the right method of starving the cells.

Finally, Wilmut and Campbell managed to produce 14 embryos. They transferred them into surrogate mothers. In July 1995, five lambs were born. Three died soon after birth, but two survived. They were named Megan and Morag. This was an important breakthrough. For the first time, animals had been cloned from embryonic cells that had been grown for several months in a laboratory.

The first cloned sheep, Megan and Morag, were born in 1995. However, Neal First had already cloned a cow from an embryonic cell in 1987, so their birth did not attract that much attention.

The birth of Dolly

Encouraged by their success with Megan and Morag, Ian Wilmut and Keith Campbell decided to try cloning an adult mammal cell. This was something that had never been achieved before. An adult cell is specialized. This means that some of its genes have been switched off. The adult cell's genetic material would have to be reprogrammed in order to produce an entire new **organism**. After many attempts, the two scientists and their team succeeded.

To produce Dolly, Wilmut and Campbell's team used the nucleus taken from an udder cell of a six-year-old Finn Dorset sheep. These sheep have white faces. The scientists injected the nucleus from one of these cells into an unfertilized egg cell which had had its nucleus removed. The unfertilized egg cell came from a Scottish blackface ewe.

A tiny pulse of electricity caused the new nucleus to fuse with the **cytoplasm** of the egg cell. This also activated the cells and made them more likely to divide.

Once Wilmut and Campbell's team had fused the cells, they needed to ensure that the resulting cell would develop into an embryo. They grew it for six or seven days in the laboratory, to see if it divided and developed into an embryo as normal. The embryo was then transferred to a surrogate mother, another Scottish blackface ewe. Six weeks before the date the lamb was due to be born, somebody was employed to sleep in the laboratory to make sure the ewe was OK. They did not want anything to go wrong at this stage!

TIMELINE

1981	Ian Wilmut begins his research on genetically modifying sheep.
June 1995	Megan and Morag, the first mammals cloned from embryonic cells, are born.
July 1996	Dolly, the first mammal cloned from an adult cell, is born.
February 1997	Dolly's birth is announced to the world.

In July 1996, a sheep was born and they called her Dolly. She had a white face, like the Finn Dorset sheep from which the two scientists had taken the cell nucleus. Dolly was the world's first clone of an adult mammal cell. This success was truly remarkable because it proved that the genetic material from a specialized adult cell, such as an udder cell, could be reprogrammed. This cell had originally been programmed to switch on only those genes needed by udder cells. However, the scientists had reprogrammed the cell so that it could produce an entire adult sheep.

Dolly was the best-known sheep in the world. In 1997, when her birth was announced, her photo appeared in newspapers and magazines around the world.

Looking for proof

After Dolly's birth, Wilmut and Campbell needed to prove that she really was a clone of the ewe from which the udder cell had been taken. They had used some udder cells that had been in the freezer for three years! The ewe from which the cells had been taken was long since dead. One piece of evidence was the fact that Dolly was a white-faced Finn Dorset sheep like the donor ewe. The next piece of evidence came from comparing the DNA of the remaining udder cells with Dolly's DNA. To Wilmut and Campbell's relief, they matched.

Dolly was looked after well. For the first few years, she lived with Megan and Morag. Visiting reporters gave her a lot of treats, which meant that she put on weight. She suffered from arthritis in her back leg and she only lived to be six years old, which is quite young for a sheep. In 2003, she had to be put down, when she developed a lung disease usually found in older sheep.

The birth of Dolly came after Ian Wilmut had spent 14 years carrying out research at the Roslin Institute. He is now Professor Wilmut and runs a regenerative medicine research centre at the University of Edinburgh, in Scotland.

Some scientists think that Dolly's short life was due to the fact that she was cloned from a six-year-old sheep who was already over halfway through her life. These scientists believe that Dolly was therefore "born middle-aged". If they are right, it is possible that the cloning process shortened her life.

When people arrived to see Dolly, she would rush up to the front of her pen and bleat loudly for attention.

Cloning – good or bad?

People reacted with surprise and curiosity when Dolly's birth was announced on 22 February 1997. There were soon headlines in newspapers around the world claiming that human cloning would be next. Many people found the idea of cloning rather worrying and frightening. Before long, people in some countries were calling for cloning research to be banned.

The United States government established a five-year ban on the use of federal money for research into human cloning while the matter was investigated further. Many other countries did the same. Scientists were concerned that all the new laws would prevent exciting discoveries being made, especially those in medical research.

? HOW DID SCIENTISTS PROVE THAT DOLLY WAS A CLONE?

Scientists proved that Dolly was really a clone by comparing her DNA to that of the remaining udder cells. They used a technique called **genetic fingerprinting**. The DNA was chopped up into fragments, using restriction enzymes, and the fragments were separated. Using a photographic technique, an image of the DNA fragments was obtained. This looked a bit like a barcode on an item from a supermarket. This barcode, or genetic fingerprint, matched that of the udder cells.

Treating disease

Wilmut and Campbell's success excited medical scientists because they thought cloning could be very useful in treating certain diseases. When cloning is used in medical treatment it is called **therapeutic** cloning. Cloning on its own cannot cure disease. But, when combined with other research (such as that on different types of cell), cloning could eventually become a powerful weapon against disease.

First clones of human embryos

In 2001, scientists from Advanced Cell Technologies (ACT), in Massachusetts, in the United States, announced that they had cloned the first human **embryos**. To do this, they collected eggs from women's **ovaries**. Then they removed the **nucleus** from each egg, using a tiny needle. A human skin cell was inserted inside the empty egg. The cells were then given a small electric shock to make them fuse together.

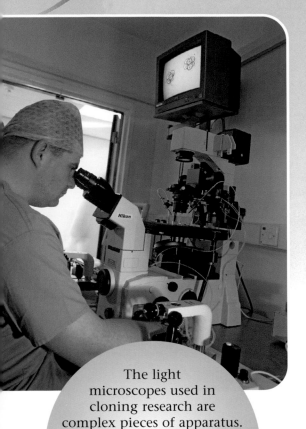

The light microscopes used in cloning research are complex pieces of apparatus. This researcher is looking down the eyepiece of a light microscope and using the micromanipulators to select a healthy embryo.

WHAT IS A MICROMANIPULATOR?

A modern cloning laboratory is equipped with a microscope and a **micromanipulator**. The specimen is placed in a small dish under the microscope. Fine, glass micro-tools are placed in the micromanipulator tool holders. The researcher can control the pressure at the tip of each micro-tool. The tool on the left holds the egg in place. The tool on the right is used to remove the nucleus from the egg and replace it with the donor nucleus.

This method was only partly successful. Out of eight eggs, three began dividing, and one divided into six cells before it stopped. As human eggs are in very short supply, the researchers could only use a small number of eggs. This is one of the main problems with therapeutic cloning.

Skin grafts

One of the first medical uses of therapeutic cloning was to treat people with bad burns. These people needed a skin graft to repair their damaged skin. Usually, the top layer of skin has to be removed from an unburnt part of the body. This unburnt skin is then used to cover the damaged area. Skin can also be obtained from **tissue** banks, where skin taken from dead **organ** donors is stored. The skin can be placed in a liquid that keeps the cells alive for about 10 days. Alternatively, the skin can be frozen, and kept for several months.

A better way is to make an artificial skin from cloned cells. Skin cells are mixed with nutrients. This mixture (a culture) is poured over a very thin plastic mesh. The cells divide and grow, forming a layer. The cells are all clones of each other. Once a large enough piece of skin has formed, it is used to cover the patient's burns.

This is a culture of skin cells that will be laid over burnt skin, to help the skin repair itself.

Finding out about stem cells

During the 1980s, scientists discovered that cloning could be usefully combined with **genetic engineering**. Then, in the late 1990s, they started to make many advances in the related field of **stem cell** research.

Stem cells were first discovered by an American scientist, called Roy Stevens, in 1953. However, little was known about these cells until Ernest McCulloch and James Till published their work on **bone marrow** and stem cells in 1963.

This stem cell is in the bone marrow. It has the ability to divide and form all the different types of blood cells, including red blood cells, white blood cells, and **platelets**.

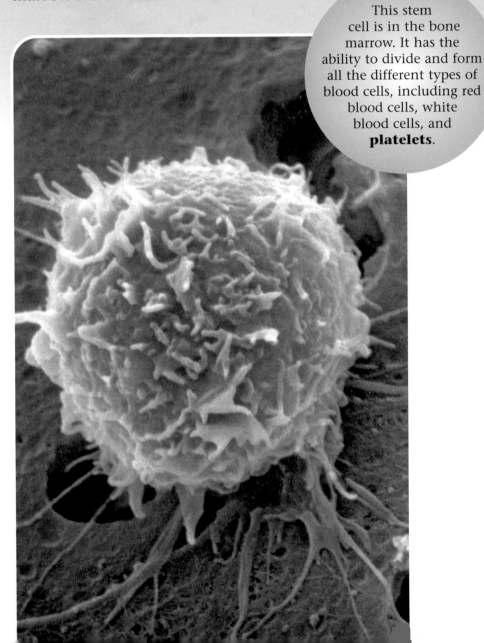

Stem cells form in an embryo that is just a few days old. Their job is to divide and form the 200 or so different types of specialized cell found in a complex **organism**, such as a human. Once a cell has become specialized to do a particular job, say as a skin cell or a muscle cell, it loses the ability to divide. But stem cells retain the ability to divide. Stem cells are found in adult humans, too. Here, they repair tissues, for example in the skin, bone marrow, and intestines. However, stem cells are nowhere near as numerous in adults as they are in embryos.

A doctor examines a man suffering from Parkinson's disease. The symptoms of Parkinson's disease include slowness of movement and trembling.

Stem cells may eventually be used to treat diseases, such as leukaemia (a type of blood **cancer**), Parkinson's disease, and **diabetes**. In 1998, two American teams, one led by James Thomson and the other by John Gearhart, managed to grow stem cells in the laboratory. This opened up the possibility of growing stem cells, and then injecting them into a patient to treat damaged tissues and organs. The stem cells would replace the damaged cells and allow the tissue to regenerate.

However, there is a problem. The body's white blood cells attack anything entering the body that is recognized as foreign. Any stem cells injected into the body would therefore be attacked and destroyed. This is called **rejection** and the only way to prevent it happening is to give the patient anti-rejection drugs.

COULD CLONING OVERCOME REJECTION?

Cloning could be used to avoid the problem of rejection. The idea is to remove a nucleus from one of the patient's own cells and transfer it to an empty egg cell. The new cell would form an embryo, and the embryo would grow stem cells. These stem cells would be grown in the laboratory and then be injected into the patient. They would not be rejected because they would carry the patient's genetic information.

Cloning rare animals and livestock

Some scientists now think that cloning could help save some of the world's rarest species. The first step towards cloning an **endangered** species took place in 2001.

Scientists at Advanced Cell Technologies (ACT) produced a gaur clone. A gaur is a rare species of wild ox. The team took cells from a male gaur's skin and inserted them into empty egg cells taken from domestic cows. The resulting **embryos** were placed in cows that were used as **surrogate** mothers.

Eight cows became pregnant, but only one baby gaur was born. The scientists called him Noah. Sadly, Noah died after 48 hours from natural causes. Although Noah died, his birth proved that this cross-species cloning technique was successful and could be used in the conservation of rare species. ACT did not repeat this experiment and no more gaurs have been cloned.

There are about 36,000 gaurs left in India and Southeast Asia. Their numbers have fallen because they are hunted by humans. They are also threatened because the forests, bamboo jungles, and grasslands where they live have been cleared.

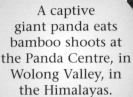

A captive giant panda eats bamboo shoots at the Panda Centre, in Wolong Valley, in the Himalayas.

Will cloning save rare animals?

Cloning rare animals will only work with species that have close relatives to supply donor eggs and provide surrogates. For example, pandas are an endangered species. But there would be little chance of successfully cloning pandas because they have no close relatives.

Many films have featured clones. In *Jurassic Park*, for instance, some scientists took **DNA** from the gut of a mosquito trapped in amber (the fossilized resin of a tree). Any mosquito from the time of the dinosaurs would have fed on dinosaur blood. In the film, the scientists took the DNA from the blood in the mosquito's gut. They then reassembled the DNA and placed it in a crocodile's egg. A dinosaur hatched out of the egg. From that one dinosaur, they succeeded in cloning many more.

? COULD SCIENTISTS REALLY BRING BACK DINOSAURS?

Although the *Jurassic Park* story sounds very far-fetched, it was partly based on recent scientific developments. At present, it is not possible to reconstruct DNA, or to extract DNA from insects trapped in amber. But who knows what will be possible in the future?

Super cows, sheep, and horses

People have been improving domestic animals for centuries through the slow process of selective breeding. The farmer chooses the animals with the best characteristics and uses them to breed the next generation. Because of this selection process, modern cows are heavier than cows in ancient times. They also produce far more milk. In the same way, domestic hens can lay as many as 320 eggs a year, compared with wild jungle fowl, which only lay about 60 eggs a year.

However, selective breeding takes time, especially with larger animals. For example, cows can only breed when they are a few years old and they usually only produce a single calf. A farmer may breed a top-class animal, but the offspring may not be as good as its parents. In this case, years of breeding may be wasted. Cloning offers breeders the chance to produce perfect copies of an animal.

These modern hens are very different from chickens in ancient times.

Most farm animal cloning is done by **nuclear transfer**. The prize animal is the source of the donor **nucleus**. This process can be used to produce any number of clones of the very best farm animals.

WILL CLONING EVER BE PROFITABLE FOR FARMERS?

In time, cloning may become more efficient and then more people will be able to afford to clone their animals. As a cloned cow is so expensive, it would never be killed for its meat. At present, the main commercial benefit would be to use the clone for breeding purposes. Once the cost of cloning comes down, dairy farmers could boost their milk production by using cows cloned from top-yielding dairy cows. However, this will only be commercially possible if the public accept food from cloned farm animals (see pages 42–43).

Too expensive

At present, cloning is expensive because the success rate is low. For example, only about 15 per cent of embryos develop successfully. The only people willing to spend as much as £50,000 per cloned animal are those who have valuable, prize-winning animals. One of the first cloned commercial cows was called Genesis, born in 2000. She was cloned from a prize-winning Holstein cow called Zita.

However, many farmers are looking to the future. They may not be able to afford to clone their animals yet. But they are asking scientists to take samples from their current prize-winning animals. The samples can then be stored for possible use in years to come.

This is a prize-winning Hereford bull. Hereford cattle are bred for their beef in the United Kingdom and the United States. Cloning an animal like this one could enable farmers to improve the quality of their entire herd.

Cloned dairy herds

In 2001, the world's first herd of cloned dairy cows started producing milk at a farm in Wisconsin, in the United States, as part of a research project. The project looked at the effect of diet on the amount of milk that was produced. Because the animals were genetically identical, any difference had to be due to their diet and not due to differences in **genes**. The researchers checked the composition of the milk produced by the cloned cows. They found that it was identical to the milk produced by other cows. This seemed to prove that cloning had not changed anything in the milk.

Nevertheless, surveys have shown that people do not like the idea of drinking milk from cloned cows. They are worried that the clones may be abnormal and their milk could be harmful to drink. Consumer groups want meat or milk from cloned animals to be clearly labelled. This would allow consumers to decide if they want to consume food and drink from a cloned animal.

These are some of the cloned cattle that were kept as part of a research project in Wisconsin. The herd was made up of 21 cows, 17 of them cloned from the same animal.

CAN RACEHORSES BE CLONED?

The first cloned horse was born in 2003. This raised a number of issues. Imagine that you own a winning racehorse and you could clone it to produce an exact copy that would also win races. At the moment, a top racehorse can be bred. However, there is no way of knowing if the offspring will be as fast as its parents. Sometimes a winning horse is infertile, and the only way it can have offspring is by cloning. At present, there are strict rules in horse racing concerning the use of **artificial insemination**, **fertility treatment**, and cloning. Any foal produced using these processes cannot be registered as a thoroughbred racehorse.

Problems ahead

Another problem is that breeders are concerned that cloning will reduce the variation amongst animals. If a prize bull is continually cloned, then the bull will father many offspring over a number of years. All the offspring will have the same male parent, so they will all have similar genes. Genetic diversity makes for a healthier herd of cattle, and cloning reduces that diversity. Genetic diversity is usually maintained by breeding animals with completely unrelated animals. This produces new combinations of genes that could benefit the animals. Farmers are also worried about scientific reports showing that cloned cows and pigs are not as healthy as normal animals and that they may die early.

As the number of cloned livestock increases in the United States, consumer groups are making their concerns known. There is currently a US government ban in place, preventing the sale of food from cloned animals. But this may change in the future.

Human cloning

In 2004, Professor Woo Suk Hwang and his team of researchers in Korea hit the headlines around the world. They announced that they had succeeded in obtaining embryonic **stem cells** from a cloned human **embryo**. The embryo had been cloned in order to produce stem cells to treat disease.

Hwang and his team said they had taken skin cells from different people with diseases that would benefit from stem cell therapy. They transferred the cells into empty human egg cells. Once embryos had formed, stem cells were grown in the laboratory, using techniques developed by researchers in the United States.

Over the following year, Hwang was treated like a celebrity both in Korea and elsewhere in the world. The scientific community was stunned when, in December 2005, Hwang admitted that many of his results had been falsified. This left the research of several other groups around the world in tatters, including that of Professor Gerald Schatten, of Pittsburgh University, in the United States. Professor Schatten co-authored a research paper with Hwang in 2005, but has since decided to withdraw his name from the paper.

? WHERE DO DONATED EGGS COME FROM?

One of the reasons that experiments into human cloning are proving so difficult is the shortage of donated eggs on which to carry out the research. Hwang had managed to obtain 242 eggs from Korean women, including members of his research team, who were willing to donate eggs for stem cell research. Other researchers have had to make do with far smaller numbers of eggs. Sources of human eggs include spare eggs from **IVF** treatment (see page 47) or from schemes where women are paid to donate their eggs.

British success

Other scientists are trying to produce human embryos in order to obtain stem cells. In May 2005, a British group at the University of Newcastle, led by Professor Alison Murdoch, announced that they had successfully cloned a human embryo. This was the first time this had been achieved by a British research team.

They had taken eggs from 11 women, removed the genetic material, and replaced it with **DNA** from embryonic stem cells. Three of the embryos lived and grew in the laboratory for three days, and one survived for five days. A vital factor in this success was the time taken to collect and manipulate the egg. The clone that lasted for five days had been collected and manipulated within 15 minutes. The next stage is to produce embryos that will live long enough for stem cells to be harvested.

Dr. Miodrag Stojkovic (left) and Professor Alison Murdoch are seen here in their laboratory in Newcastle. Professor Alison Murdoch believes that it will take several years before patients can be treated with their own stem cells.

Reproductive cloning

The Newcastle group, led by Professor Alison Murdoch, were carrying out **therapeutic** cloning, as the aim of the experiment was to obtain stem cells to treat disease.

Another way in which cloning techniques could be used is to help infertile couples have children. This is called reproductive cloning. The embryo would be produced in the same way but it would then be placed in a woman's **uterus**, where it could develop into a baby.

Some women cannot produce healthy eggs, so a donor's egg could be used. The **nucleus** would be removed from the egg, and replaced with a nucleus taken from the woman or her partner. The child would be a clone of one of the parents.

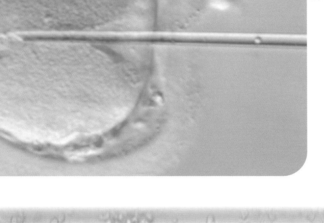

A human egg is injected with a hollow micro-needle containing a single sperm. This in vitro fertilization (IVF) method is known as intra-cytoplasmic sperm injection (ICSI).

KEVIN EGGAN'S STORY

Kevin Eggan is Assistant Professor of Molecular and Cellular Biology at Harvard University, in the United States. He puts his success in science down to his determination. His first research project involved cloning mice. He worked in the laboratory seven days a week, for a year, and still he kept on failing. He managed to make an embryo, but he could not get the embryo to grow. However, he did not give up. He just kept on trying. He likened it to a video game. The game presents you with a challenge, which you have to get past before you can get to the next level. His determination eventually paid off and he succeeded in producing cloned mice. He will need all his enthusiasm and determination for his next project, which involves cloning human cells to produce stem cells.

A lot of people are very worried by the idea of reproductive cloning. Some are concerned that human clones could suffer a number of health problems. Others believe that this type of research is morally wrong (see pages 48–49).

WHAT IS IVF?

In 1978, Louise Brown, the world's first "test tube baby", conceived through in vitro fertilization (IVF), was born in the United Kingdom. Since then, many infertile couples have had IVF treatment in order to conceive a child. First, the woman has **hormone** treatment so that she produces more eggs than normal. A very fine needle is passed through the wall of the uterus into the **ovary** to collect the eggs. The eggs are then placed in a dish. Here, sperm are added and the eggs are **fertilized**. The fertilized eggs develop into embryos and grow for a few days. Then they are checked to make sure they are healthy. Two or three embryos are placed in the woman's uterus. One or more embryos may develop into babies, though sometimes none of them develop successfully. Any spare eggs and embryos left after the procedure may be donated for research purposes.

Kevin Eggan wants to understand how nuclear transplantation actually works and to use stem cells to study illnesses such as Parkinson's disease and **Alzheimer's**.

Healthy clones?

One of the reasons why so many people are against human cloning is the concern that the clone may not be healthy. Many people think that Dolly died early for a sheep because she was a clone. Some cloned cows have had problems after birth. Researchers have discovered abnormal livers, lungs, hearts, and blood vessels. Often the cloned animals are sickly and they suffer from diseases and die early.

Imagine how the public would react if researchers produced a cloned baby that was sickly and did not live very long. People would see this as terribly cruel. They would be outraged and horrified. Until these concerns have been investigated, it would be wrong to try to clone a person.

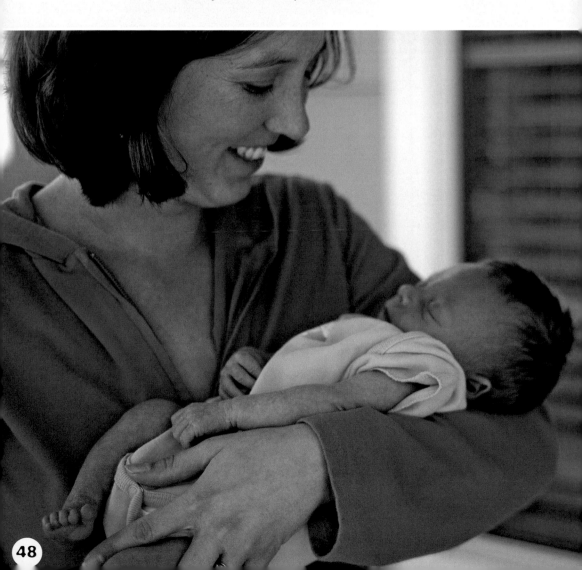

Some scientists feel that the clones' health problems are mainly caused by using adult cells as the source of the genetic material. During an individual's life, the DNA in the cells accumulates faults, called mutations. The cloning process transfers these mutations to the embryo. This could mean that a clone has a shortened lifespan or a greater risk of getting **cancer** in later life.

Concerns over human cloning

Human cloning has caused considerable debate. Some people argue that a cloned embryo only exists because it was produced in a laboratory. They say it is not a life, simply a ball of cells that cannot survive very long. Therefore it is acceptable to carry out research on these cells. In the United Kingdom, an embryo used for research has to be destroyed after 14 days. Many people feel that, as long as the 14-day rule is followed and the embryos are used for therapeutic cloning only, this research should be permitted.

Other groups do not want human embryos to be used at all. They believe that life starts with fertilization, so an embryo has the potential to develop into a new human being. They feel that destroying an embryo is like killing a person.

A mother holds her newborn son. Public opinion would not allow human cloning to go ahead if it put the baby's health at risk.

Before he was discredited, Professor Woo Suk Hwang and his team wanted to see whether they could avoid the need for human egg donors by using cows' eggs instead. Other research teams are also working on this idea. For example, researchers in China have obtained embryonic stem cells by fusing human cells with empty egg cells from rabbits. However, they could not get the stem cells to grow in the laboratory. If this research is successful in the future, it could help to resolve some of the moral concerns that people have about human cloning.

What would happen if a human clone were born?

If a human clone were ever born, many issues would be raised. Firstly, the clone would be an identical copy of somebody else. This could cause problems. For example, if the original person was a well-known sportsperson or a gifted musician, people would expect the clone to be gifted in the same way and to follow the same career path. However, the clone might have a different personality and not want to be like the original.

Secondly, wealthy people suffering from a disease might pay for a clone of themselves just to prolong their own lives. They might not care for the child as a proper parent would. They might plan to use some of the child's cells or even some of its **organs** for their own treatment.

Thirdly, animal clones are owned by the companies whose researchers have produced them. These companies have invested a lot of money in producing the clones and they want to protect their research. Would a company therefore have the right to own a human clone?

TALKING SCIENCE

"Are we really willing to sacrifice hundreds of embryos – developing human beings – to make one baby who may suffer monstrous consequences?"
Dr. David Stevens, of the Christian Medical and Dental Society, quoted in *Christian World News*, 1998

Banning research

Many governments believe that the only way to prevent human reproductive cloning is to ban all forms of human cloning. In 2005, at a meeting of the United Nations (UN), the United States called for a ban on all forms of human cloning. But UN delegates voted to put off this ban for at least two years. Without UN guidelines, individual countries can regulate human cloning as they wish. In the United States, some states have passed laws banning human cloning and scientists cannot get government funding for research into human cloning.

It is difficult to stop scientists carrying out research into cloning. If one country bans it, they may move to another country where it is not banned. However, at some point in the future, somebody, somewhere, will probably succeed in cloning a human.

TALKING SCIENCE

"We're fighting for research, and we're defending people's reproductive rights... I realize my clone would be my identical twin, and my identical twin has a right to be born."
Randolfe Wicker, founder of Clones' Rights United Front

Three cloning specialists take part in an international conference on human cloning in Washington, D.C., in the United States, in 2001.

51

Breakthroughs in cloning

A lot of research is being done on **therapeutic** cloning. Some of this research may well lead to medical advances. Cloning may also be used to produce a wide range of **genetically engineered** animals – for farming and for **organ** transplantation.

Treating diseases

One exciting branch of therapeutic cloning research is directed at treating motor neurone disease (MND). This disease attacks the nerve cells that carry messages to the muscles. As the nerve cells get damaged, the person's muscles become weaker.

Professor Ian Wilmut, head of the team that produced Dolly the sheep, and Professor Christopher Shaw, of London University, are working together on this research. They plan to take a cell **nucleus** from a person with MND and place the nucleus in an empty human egg. They will allow an **embryo** to develop and then they will remove **stem cells** from it, and grow them in the laboratory.

A scientist removes cell samples from a **gene** bank in France. Each test tube contains about 1 million cells. The cells were taken from patients affected by genetic diseases and will be studied in order to find the genes responsible for these disorders.

The stem cells will be grown in a liquid that is full of nutrients. By carefully altering the amounts of the various nutrients, they hope to be able to change the stem cells into nerve cells. Then Wilmut and Shaw will transplant the nerve cells into the patient, where they will replace the damaged nerve cells.

Cloning could also perhaps be used to help save some rare plants. For example, a new **DNA** bank has been set up in Brazil, to preserve the genetic material of **endangered** plants. Scientists plan to collect at least 1,000 plant species each year to deposit in the bank. Samples of plants will be dried out and some of their DNA extracted. The DNA samples will then be frozen and stored. In the future, this DNA could be used to clone plants that are at risk of becoming extinct. The cloned plants would then be grown and, if possible, re-established in the wild.

The DNA bank could help save some of these rare Brazilian rainforest plants for future generations.

Designer transplants

Surgeons can now carry out very complex **transplant** operations to replace damaged organs. However, there are too few organs available. There is also a very long waiting list of sick people, with those in greatest need at the top of the list. Another problem is that the donated organ has to be matched to the recipient.

Because there is a shortage of human donors, doctors are hoping to use organs from animals such as pigs. However, the patient's **immune system** would recognize the new organ as foreign and attack it. Scientists plan to genetically engineer the pigs so that their organs will not be rejected. Cloning would then be used to produce other identical pigs, which could also donate organs for transplant.

Cloning yesterday, today, and tomorrow

Cloning has come a long way since Hans Driesch first divided a sea urchin **embryo** in the 1890s. Until the 1950s, cloning experiments attracted little attention outside the scientific community. But, since the 1980s, people have come to fear the word cloning and even associate it with monsters from science fiction. Now public opinion is deeply divided. Some people believe that cloning research should be allowed because it could lead to medical advances. Meanwhile, others feel that it should be banned completely.

TALKING SCIENCE

"It is absolutely inevitable that groups are going to try to clone a human being. But they are going to create a lot of dead and dying babies along the way."

Thomas Murray, President of the Hastings Center, in New York, quoted in *USA Today* (2003)

The debate over human cloning will continue into the future, and can only intensify as technological advances make a human clone more likely.

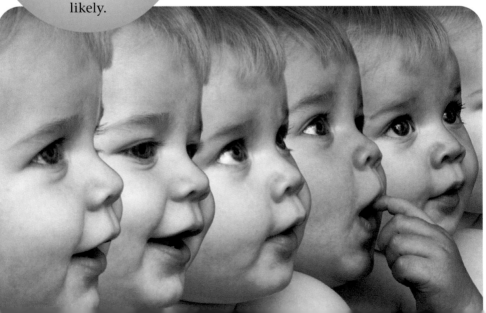

Dr Brigitte Boisselier (left) and Raël (right), of the Raëlians, hold a press conference in Canada, in 2000, to publicize their human cloning project.

Changing nature?

People who do not like the idea of cloning often say that scientists are "playing God" because they are changing living **organisms** in the laboratory. They consider it to be unnatural. Others argue that cloning takes place in the natural world, and that people have been changing plants and animals for thousands of years, using selective breeding methods. They see cloning as just another harmless step along the same path. They feel that if cloning is used carefully it could help the human race.

Human clones

A number of fertility specialists and even members of a religious movement are racing ahead, trying to be the first to create a human clone. Correct scientific procedures are not always followed. For instance, a group calling themselves the Raëlians gained worldwide publicity in 2002, when they claimed that they had helped bring the first human clone into the world. However, this claim remains unproven and practically every expert considers it a hoax.

Many people feel that cloning is among the most important scientific discoveries of the 20th century. A number of cloning specialists have been awarded Nobel Prizes in recognition of their contributions to science. The impact of cloning and related developments, such as **genetic engineering** and **stem cell** research, will probably be felt long into the 21st century. Many scientists believe that far more still remains to be achieved.

Timeline

1890s Hans Driesch divides a sea urchin embryo into two parts. Both pieces grow into sea urchins.

1901 Hans Spemann splits a two-cell newt embryo into two parts and produces two identical newts.

1914 Hans Spemann carries out a simple nuclear transfer experiment using a newt embryo.

1938 Hans Spemann proposes his "fantastical experiment". He wanted to take a nucleus from an adult cell, and place it in an egg cell that had had its own nucleus removed. He wanted to see if he could get the egg cell with its new nucleus to grow into an adult.

1952 Robert Briggs and Tom King clone northern leopard frogs.

1953 Francis Crick and James Watson work out the structure of DNA.

1962 John Gurdon announces that he has cloned a clawed toad, using the nucleus of an adult frog's gut cell.

1963 J.B.S. Haldane uses the term "clone" in a speech.

1967 DNA ligase, the enzyme that joins together strands of DNA, is isolated.

1977 Karl Illmensee claims to have produced mice with a single parent.

1978 Louise Brown, the first "test tube baby", is conceived through in vitro fertilization, and is born in the United Kingdom.

1979 Karl Illmensee claims to have cloned three mice.

1982 Davor Solter and James McGrath try to clone mice using their own version of the nuclear transfer method. They conclude that once an embryo reaches the two-cell stage it cannot be used for cloning.

1982 First mother-to-mother human embryo transfer is carried out in Melbourne, Australia. A woman who could not produce healthy eggs has a donor egg fertilized by her partner. The embryo is then placed in her uterus.

1984 Steen Willadsen clones a sheep from embryonic cells, the first example of mammal cloning using nuclear transfer.

1985 Steen Willadsen clones prize cattle embryos.

1987 Neal First, Randall Prather, and Willard Eyestone announce that they have used early embryonic cells to clone a cow.

1995 Megan and Morag the sheep, the first two mammals cloned from embryonic cells grown in the laboratory, are born at the Roslin Institute, in Scotland.

1996 Dolly the sheep, the first mammal ever to be cloned from adult cells, is born at the Roslin Institute.

1997 Dolly the sheep's birth is officially announced.

1998 Nineteen European nations sign a ban on human cloning.

1998 The Food and Drug Administration in the United States announces that it has authority to regulate human cloning.

2001 Advanced Cell Technology (ACT) announces the birth of Noah, a baby gaur clone, but he dies a few days later.

2001 British House of Commons votes to allow research on human embryos for therapeutic cloning.

2001 Scientists from ACT announce that they have cloned the first human embryos for therapeutic research. Only one embryo was able to divide into six cells before it died.

2001 World's first herd of cloned dairy cows starts producing milk at a farm in the United States.

2003 Death of Dolly the sheep is announced.

2003 First cloned horse is born.

2004 Woo Suk Hwang announces that he has managed to carry out nuclear transfer, using human egg cells, to produce embryos. His team of researchers have extracted stem cells from these embryos. However, in 2005 he admits that the results were falsified.

2005 Professor Alison Murdoch's team at Newcastle University, in the United Kingdom, announce that they have cloned a human embryo, a first for a British research group.

Biographies

These are some of the leading scientists in the story of cloning.

Robert William Briggs (1911–1983)

Robert Briggs was born in Watertown, Massachusetts, in the United States, in 1911. He went to Boston University to study business administration and then education. He graduated in 1934 with a degree in science and then went to Harvard University. In 1938, he moved to the Zoology Department at McGill University, Canada, where he studied cancerous growths in frogs. He then moved to the Lankenau Hospital Research Institute, in Philadelphia, where he focused on the role of the nucleus in the development of frogs. He worked with Thomas King to develop the technique of transferring a nucleus into an empty frog's egg. In 1952, they carried out the first successful nuclear transplantation. In 1956, Briggs became Professor of Zoology at Indiana University, where he researched inheritance and development in amphibians.

Hans Adolf Eduard Driesch (1867–1941)

Hans Driesch was born in Bad Kreuznach, Germany. He went to the University of Jena in 1889 to study zoology. During the 1890s, he worked at the Marine Zoology Station in Naples, Italy, where he studied embryology. He carried out a number of experiments on sea urchin eggs, including one in which he pulled apart the two cells of an embryo and found that each developed into a normal sea urchin. After 1900, his main interest was philosophy. He moved to the University of Heidelberg, Germany, in 1912, where he wrote several books on philosophy.

Alison Murdoch

Alison Murdoch is Professor of Reproductive Medicine, at the BioScience Centre, Newcastle, in the United Kingdom. This department was founded by Professor Murdoch in 1991. Under her leadership, it has grown to become the leading fertility centre in England. In 2004, Murdoch and her colleague, Dr. Miodrag Stojkovic, were granted the first licence in the United Kingdom to clone human embryos for therapeutic purposes. In 2005, they became the first scientists to produce a human embryo in the United Kingdom. Professor Murdoch is Chairman of the British Fertility Society.

Hans Spemann
(1869–1941)

Hans Spemann was born in Stuttgart, Germany, in 1869. After he left school, he spent some time working before going to the University of Heidelberg in 1891 to study medicine. In 1894, he moved to the University of Würzburg to take a degree in zoology, botany, and physics. In 1901, he managed to split a two-cell newt embryo into two parts to produce two clones. In 1908, he became Professor of Zoology and Comparative Anatomy at Rostock. In 1914, he carried out the first nuclear transfer experiment on a newt embryo. In 1919, he was appointed Professor of Zoology at the University of Freiburg-im-Breisgau, where he continued his research for another 20 years. He was awarded a Nobel Prize in 1935. In 1938, he published his book, *Embryonic Development and Induction*, in which he described his research.

Ian Wilmut

Ian Wilmut was born near Warwick, in the United Kingdom, in 1944. He went to Nottingham University, where he studied agricultural science. Later, he moved to Cambridge University, where he obtained his doctorate in 1971. His research on embryology led to the birth of the first calf from a frozen embryo in 1973. In 1974, he moved to Edinburgh to work at the Animal Breeding Research Station, later called the Roslin Institute. In early 1996, Wilmut and his team at Roslin first succeeded in producing a pair of lambs, Megan and Morag, from embryonic cells. Later that year, the team produced Dolly the sheep, the world's first cloned mammal. Wilmut stayed at the Roslin Institute until March 2005, when he joined the Research Institute for Medical Cell Biology at the University of Edinburgh. In 1999, he became a member of the Order of the British Empire (OBE). In 2000, he was elected a Fellow of the Royal Society of Edinburgh.

Glossary

Alzheimer's progressive, incurable disease that destroys brain cells, gradually causing memory loss

artificial insemination process in which semen containing sperm is placed in a female's uterus by artificial means

asexual reproduction form of reproduction in which there is a single parent organism and all the offspring are identical to the parent

bacterium single-celled organism that does not have a nucleus

base four chemicals (adenine, thymine, cytosine, and guanine) arranged in a sequence, to make up a particular gene

bone marrow liquid-like tissue found in the centre of the body's largest bones

cancer disease in which cells multiply abnormally and form a growth called a tumour

chromosome thread-like structure in the cell's nucleus, made up of DNA and protein

cytoplasm jelly-like substance that fills a cell

diabetes disease caused by the pancreas failing to produce enough insulin

DNA (deoxyribonucleic acid) molecule that carries a living thing's genetic information

embryo new individual that forms when an egg is fertilized

endangered (of a species) at risk of becoming extinct

enzyme protein used in a cell to control and speed up chemical reactions

fertility treatment method used to improve fertility or increase the likelihood of pregnancy

fertilization process in which the nuclei of a sperm and an egg fuse to make a new living thing

gamete sex cell (e.g. egg or sperm) of a living thing

gene unit of inheritance that is passed on from parent to offspring, made up of a length of DNA

genetic code sequence of bases along a length of DNA that forms the genetic code. This code contains the instructions needed to make proteins.

genetic engineering process of altering a living thing's DNA

genetic fingerprinting process of chopping DNA into fragments using restriction enzymes. The fragments are separated, then labelled with radioactive markers.

hormone chemical messenger in the body

immune system body's defences, including white blood cells, which recognize and attack foreign organisms, such as bacteria and viruses

in vitro fertilization (IVF) process in which a woman's egg is fertilized in a glass dish ("in vitro" means "in glass") in a laboratory

leukaemia cancer of the blood that affects white blood cells

membrane thin barrier, made of protein and fat, around a cell

metamorphosis change in form that occurs when an animal, such as a frog, changes from larva to adult

micromanipulator apparatus used with a light microscope to handle embryos and other microscopic structures

molecule smallest particle of a substance that still has all the properties of the substance, made up of one or more atoms

nucleus central part of a cell that contains DNA and controls many cell functions

nuclear transfer process in which the nucleus is removed from the donor cell and placed in an empty egg cell

organ part of the body made up of different tissues, such as the heart or liver

organism living thing

ovary female reproductive organ that produces eggs

platelet type of blood cell that is involved in blood clotting

rejection reaction that occurs when the body's defences attack a transplant

sexual reproduction process in which two sex cells, usually an egg and a sperm, fuse to form one fertilized cell

stem cell cell that retains the ability to divide and to form a variety of specialized cells, such as blood cells and nerve cells

surrogate female animal that has an embryo implanted in her uterus

therapeutic used to treat disease

tissue group of cells of the same type that work together to carry out a specific role, such as muscle tissue or liver tissue

transplant living tissue that is moved from one part of the body to another, or tissue that is moved from one person's body to another

uterus female organ, also known as a womb, in which the unborn child grows and develops

Further resources

If you have enjoyed this book and want to find out more, you can look at the following books and websites.

Books

21st Century Citizen:
Genetic Engineering
Paul Dowswell
(Franklin Watts, 2004)

Genetic Engineering – The Facts
Sally Morgan
(Evans Brothers, 2002)

Science at the Edge: Cloning
Sally Morgan
(Heinemann Library, 2002)

Usborne Internet-Linked
Introduction to Genes and DNA
Anna Claybourne
(Usborne, 2003)

Websites

Genetic Science Learning
Centre: Cloning in Focus
gslc.genetics.utah.edu/units/
cloning/index.cfm
Excellent website with information on all aspects of biotechnology, including cloning, explained with diagrams and photos.

Biotechnology online
www.biotechnologyonline.gov.au
Australian biotechnology resource for secondary school pupils.

Bioscience Information
Gateway for the European
Public and Information
Practitioners
www.ecod-bio.org/main.htm
A website that provides information on biosciences, answers to many frequently asked questions, and good-quality educational materials.

Cloning Fact Sheet
www.ornl.gov/sci/techresources/
Human_Genome/elsi/cloning.shtml
Web page with well-explained information and links to many articles on cloning.

Stem Cell Information
stemcells.nih.gov
The official National Institute of Health resource for stem cell research.

How Stuff Works
science.howstuffworks.com/
cloning.htm
Websites of the major science journals and newspapers, featuring stem cells articles from publications including *New Scientist*, *Science*, *Focus*, and the *Guardian*.

Index

Index

Titles in the *Chain Reactions* series include:

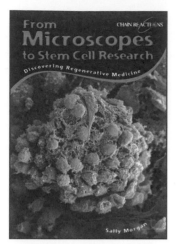

Hardback   0 431 18593 X

Hardback   0 431 18594 8

Hardback   0 431 18595 6

Hardback   0 431 18596 4

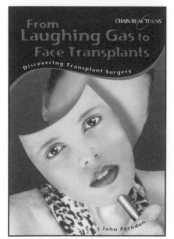

Hardback   0 431 18597 2

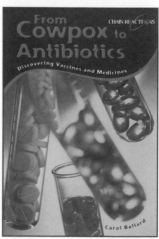

Hardback   0 431 18598 0

Find out about other titles from Heinemann Library on our website www.heinemann.co.uk/library